Author's N

This book features 100 influential and inspiring quotes by Lao Tzu. Undoubtedly, this collection will give you a huge boost of inspiration.

COPYRIGHT © 2021 DAVID SMITH

1

"From wonder into wonder existence opens."

2

"The best fighter is never angry."

3

"If you do not change direction, you may end up where you are heading."

4

"The snow goose need not bathe to make itself white. Neither need you do anything but be yourself."

5

"Knowing others is intelligence; knowing yourself is true wisdom. Mastering others is strength; mastering yourself is true power."

6

"Knowledge is a treasure, but practice is the key to it."

7

"To a mind that is still the whole universe surrenders."

8

"Those who know do not speak.
Those who speak do not know."

9

"Be like water."

10

"To understand the limitation of things, desire them."

11

"Be still. Stillness reveals the secrets of eternity."

12

"Respond intelligently even to unintelligent treatment."

13

"There is a time to live and a time to die but never to reject the moment."

14

"To know that you do not know is the best.
To think you know when you do not is a disease.
Recognizing this disease as a disease is to be free of it."

15

"Because of a great love, one is courageous."

16

"An over sharpened sword cannot last long."

17

"Watch your thoughts, they become your words; watch your words, they become your actions; watch your actions, they become your habits; watch your habits, they become your character; watch your character, it becomes your destiny."

18

"When you accept yourself, the whole world accepts you."

19

"Sincere words are not fine; fine words are not sincere."

20

"The way of heaven is to help and not harm."

21

"Music in the soul can be heard by the universe."

22

"He who talks more is sooner exhausted."

23

"Time is a created thing. To say 'I don't have time,' is like saying, 'I don't want to.'"

24

"As soon as you have made a thought, laugh at it."

25

"A scholar who cherishes the love of comfort is not fit to be deemed a scholar."

26

"A man with outward courage dares to die; a man with inner courage dares to live."

27

"One who is too insistent on his own views finds few to agree with him."

28

"A bad man is a good man's job."

29

"Love is of all the passions the strongest, for it attacks simultaneously the head, the heart, and the senses."

30

"When the student is ready the teacher will appear. When the student is truly ready... The teacher will disappear."

31

"Being deeply loved by someone gives you strength, while loving someone deeply gives you courage."

32

"Take care with the end as you do with the beginning."

33

"The further one goes, the less one knows."

34

"When goodness is lost there is morality."

35

"To hold, you must first open your hand. Let go."

36

"A good traveler has no fixed plans and is not intent on arriving."

37

"Stop thinking, and end your problems."

38

"If you are depressed you are living in the past."

39

"If you are anxious you are living in the future.
If you are at peace you are living in the present."

40

"When there is no desire, all things are at peace."

41

"The more laws and order are made prominent, the more thieves and robbers there will be."

42

"If you try to change it, you will ruin it. Try to hold it, and you will lose it."

43

"Stop leaving and you will arrive. Stop searching and you will see. Stop running away and you will be found."

44

"He who obtains has little. He who scatters has much."

45

"If you want to lead them you must place yourself behind them."

46

"Give evil nothing to oppose and it will disappear by itself."

47

"Those who flow as life flows know they need no other force."

48

"He who acts, spoils; he who grasps, lets slip."

49

"If you wish to be out front,
then act as if you were behind."

50

"To attain knowledge, add things everyday. To attain wisdom, remove things every day."

51

"Become totally empty.
Quiet the restlessness of the mind
only then will you witness everything unfolding from emptiness."

52

"If you realize that all things change, there is nothing you will try to hold on to. If you are not afraid of dying, there is nothing you cannot achieve."

53

"Care about what other people think and you will always be their prisoner."

54

"Life is a series of natural and spontaneous changes. Don't resist them; that only creates sorrow. Let reality be reality. Let things flow naturally forward in whatever way they like."

55

"The Tao is nowhere to be found. Yet it nourishes and completes all things."

56

"When men lost their understanding of the Tao, intelligence came along, bringing hypocrisy with it."

57

"Manifest plainness, Embrace simplicity, Reduce selfishness, Have few desires."

58

"Be content with what you have; rejoice in the way things are. When you realize there is nothing lacking, the whole world belongs to you."

59

"The key to growth is the introduction of higher dimensions of consciousness into our awareness."

60

"Kindness in words creates confidence. Kindness in thinking creates profoundness. Kindness in giving creates love."

61

"Because one believes in oneself, one doesn't try to convince others. Because one is content with oneself, one doesn't need others' approval. Because one accepts oneself, the whole world accepts him or her."

62

"At the center of your being you have the answer; you know who you are and you know what you want."

63

"Be gentle and you can be bold; be frugal and you can be liberal; avoid putting yourself before others and you can become a leader among men."

64

"I have just three things to teach: simplicity, patience, compassion. These three are your greatest treasures."

65

"If you understand others you are smart.
If you understand yourself you are illuminated.
If you overcome others you are powerful."

66

"Colors blind the eye
Sounds deafen the ear.
Flavors numb the taste.
Thoughts weaken the mind.
Desires wither the heart."

67

"Respond to anger with virtue. Deal with difficulties while they are still easy. Handle the great while it is still small."

68

"Trying to control the future is like trying to take the master carpenter's place. When you handle the master carpenter's tools, chances are that you'll cut your hand."

69

"Be careful what you water your dreams with. Water them with worry and fear and you will produce weeds that choke the life from your dream. Water them with optimism and solutions and you will cultivate success."

70

"If a person seems wicked, do not cast him away. Awaken him with your words, elevate him with your deeds, repay his injury with your kindness. Do not cast him away; cast away his wickedness."

71

"Love is a decision – not an emotion!"

72

"Go to the people. Live with them, learn from them, love them."

73

"Your own positive future begins in this moment. All you have is right now. Every goal is possible from here."

74

"If lightning is the anger of the gods, then the gods are concerned mostly about trees."

75

"Health is the greatest possession. Contentment is the greatest treasure. Confidence is the greatest friend."

76

"If you do not value rare treasures, you will stop others from stealing."

77

"A violent wind does not last for a whole morning; a sudden rain does not last for the whole day."

78

"There is no disaster greater than not being content; there is no misfortune greater than being covetous."

79

"Water is the softest thing, yet it can penetrate mountains and earth. This shows clearly the principle of softness overcoming hardness."

80

"The reason why the universe is eternal is that it does not live for itself; it gives life to others as it transforms."

81

"Ordinary men hate solitude. But the Master makes use of it, embracing his aloneness, realizing he is one with the whole universe."

82

"Do you have the patience to wait until your mud settles and the water is clear?"

83

"Do you imagine the universe is agitated? Go into the desert at night and look at the stars. This practice should answer the question."

84

"So the unwanting soul
sees what's hidden,
and the ever-wanting soul
sees only what it wants."

85

"When wealth and honors lead to arrogancy, this brings its evil on itself."

86

"Countless words count less than the silent balance between yin and yang."

87

"Governing a great nation is like cooking a small fish – too much handling will spoil it."

88

"Hope and fear are both phantoms that arise from thinking of the self. When we don't see the self as self, what do we have to fear?"

89

"I do not concern myself with gods and spirits either good or evil nor do I serve any."

90

"He who defends with love will be secure; Heaven will save him, and protect him with love."

91

"Just remain in the center; watching. And then forget that you are there."

92

"In dwelling, live close to the ground. In thinking, keep to the simple. In conflict, be fair and generous. In governing, don't try to control. In work, do what you enjoy. In family life, be completely present."

93

"The Wise Man is square but not sharp, honest but not not malign, straight but not severe, bright but not dazzling."

94

"The softest things in the world overcome the hardest things in the world. Through this I know the advantage of taking no action."

95

"The hard and mighty lie beneath the ground
While the tender and weak dance on the breeze above."

96

"Spring comes, and the grass grows by itself."

97

"Do not conquer the world with force, for force only causes resistance. Thorns spring up when an army passes. Years of misery follow a great victory. Do only what needs to be done without using violence."

98

"The master observes the world but trusts his inner vision. He allows things to come and go. He prefers what is within to what is without."

99

"If the people must be ever fearful of death, then there will always be an executioner."

100

"Our enemies are not demons, but human beings like ourselves."

Made in the USA
Monee, IL
10 October 2024